Flossie and the Pirate's Gold

By

Stephen Dignall

First paperback edition: 2025
ISBN 978-1-7384918-3-4
Published by: McStay

McStay

Dedicated to: "Flossie the Cat"
The inspiration for this story.

Flossie the cat was so cozy and snug, fast asleep on her raggedy rug.
Dad took one look and said, 'Won't someone please, throw out this old rug it's infested with fleas!'

But Flossie knew what no one could see,
this rug held magic—so wild and so
free.
One little twitch, then a sudden surprise,
as upward it soared to silvery skies!

Onwards and upwards past rooftops and trees, gliding so soft on the gentlest of breeze.
Over towns and cities, fields, sea and foam, 'Oh dear,' thought Flossie, 'I'm so far from home!

Through stormy winds and blustery gales, until she spotted a big ship with sails!
Closer they flew until she could see, a skull and crossbones! 'Oh no, I must flee!'

With a bump and a thud, they land with a bang, waking the crew, such a villainous gang.
Before she could hide, she was quickly found, 'The Captain will know what to do, I'll be bound!'

With pistols and swords, they circled around, but brave little Flossie just stood her ground.
The first mate just chuckled and showing no pity, 'it's walking the plank time for you little kitty!

The Captain arrived and said, 'This cat can stay, but only if she can catch rats for her pay!'
Down below decks she was clever and quick, and soon there were no more rats left on the ship.

Young Puss,' said the Captain, 'you've done a great job, you've now earned the right to join my scurvy mob. This map that I'm holding, though tattered and old, will guide us to treasure, or so I've been told!

'Land ahoy!' Cried the lookout, and sounded the bell. The pirates cheered loudly, 'tis gold we do smell.'

Splish splash went the oars as they rowed to the shore, the pirates all landed with a ferocious roar. 'Take two-hundred paces, then four to the right, then you must start digging with all of your might!'

Clink clank went the spades, what was it they'd found? A treasure chest buried six feet under ground!
They opened the trunk and to their great surprise, gold, silver and diamonds brought gleams to their eyes.

They all gave a cheer, shouting, 'Hip, hip, hip hoorah,' for Flossie the cat who had brought them this far.
The captain declared 'She's the best cat we've had, before she arrived all our luck has been bad.

'As a crew member, she must have her share, of treasure we found or it wouldn't be fair.'
But the rug became restless, the time was at hand, to bid a farewell to this black-hearted band.

Goodbye & Good Luck!

The rug floated gently then took to the air, the pirates all shouting, 'Young pussy take care!'
Her adventure now over she lay on the rug, until she was back in her kitchen so snug.

Stretching her legs and licking her pads, thinking about all the fun she'd just had. When Sally saw Flossie, she gasped in surprise, 'What's this on the floor before my very eyes?'
Two bright shiny coins so golden and round, were lying right next to her rug on the ground!

Sal picked up the coins, then, scratching her head, asked, 'Where is it you go to while I'm in my bed?' Flossie just yawned, purring contentedly, 'A pirate's life's fun, but it's not right for me!'

Questions for young Pirates:

What would you do if you found yourself on a pirate ship like Flossie did?

Why do you think the pirates decided to let Flossie stay on their ship?

How did Flossie help the pirates, and why were they so happy with her?

What do you think Flossie learned from her adventure with the pirates?

If you had a magical rug like Flossie's, where would you go and why?

How do you think Sally felt when she found the golden doubloon?

Do you think Flossie will go on another adventure? What might happen next?

If you could be a pirate for a day, what would you want to find in a treasure chest?

www.ingramcontent.com/pod-product-compliance
Lightning Source LLC
Chambersburg PA
CBHW042103040426

42448CB00002B/118